OXFORD

CHORAL
CLASSICS

English Church Music

Volume 1: Anthems and Motets

EDITED BY ROBERT KING

SERIES EDITOR
JOHN RUTTER

MUSIC DEPARTMENT

OXFORD
UNIVERSITY PRESS

OXFORD
UNIVERSITY PRESS

Great Clarendon Street, Oxford OX2 6DP, England

Oxford University Press is a department of the University of Oxford.
It furthers the University's aim of excellence in research, scholarship,
and education by publishing worldwide

Oxford is a registered trade mark of Oxford University Press
in the UK and in certain other countries

This collection © Oxford University Press 2010

Database right Oxford University Press (maker)

Robert King and John Rutter have asserted their right under the Copyright,
Designs and Patents Act, 1988, to be identified as the Editors of these works

First published 2010

1 3 5 7 9 10 8 6 4 2

ISBN 978-0-19-336841-5

Music originated in Sibelius
Printed in Great Britain on acid-free paper by
Halstan & Co. Ltd, Amersham, Bucks

CONTENTS

* In order to minimize page turns, these anthems have been placed out of alphabetical order.

PREFACE

The aim of the *Oxford Choral Classics* series is to offer choirs a practical and inexpensive working library of standard repertoire in new, reliable editions. The majority of works are classics of the repertoire, but also included are pieces of music that are less widely known but are of especial value. Inevitably, any such anthology reflects the personal perspective of its editor, and for this volume of English church music in particular, for which there is such a fine and varied range of repertoire from across more than five centuries, the available selection is exceptionally rich and could easily have filled several volumes. Cornerstones of the repertoire, such as Byrd's *Haec Dies* and *Sing joyfully*, Stanford's *Beati quorum via*, Harris's *Faire is the heaven*, and Purcell's *Remember not, Lord, our offences*, are set alongside less frequently performed works such as Patrick Hadley's wonderful *My song is love unknown*, Purcell's melancholy *Let mine eyes run down with tears*, and Wesley's *Praise the Lord, O my soul*. This last anthem was an especial joy to discover afresh, for its concluding movement is often performed but is only an extract from a much larger work. This volume allows choirs the option to perform either the full work or just the well-known extract. Returning to original sources has produced some fascinating variants: the many singers who will know Howells's eloquent *Like as the hart* can finally see the composer's original thoughts for the soprano descant that decorates the return of the opening theme, and can then choose between that early setting or the more frequently heard version.

The specific parameters followed have been these:

1. The period covered ranges from around 1500 to the present day, although copyright considerations have limited the scope and amount of twentieth-century music included. A parallel intention has been to present a representative selection of music from each century.

2. Pieces originally intended to have orchestral accompaniment, rather than organ, have been excluded, hence the omission of the rich seam of Restoration verse anthems with strings by Purcell and his contemporaries, of Elizabethan works originally intended to be accompanied by viol consort, and of eighteenth-century works by Handel and his contemporaries (resulting in a relative dearth of music from that century in this volume). None of these categories of anthem sound as well in organ transcription as they do in their original instrumental versions. However, both Mendelssohn's famous *Hear my prayer* and Hadley's *My song is love unknown* exist with the composer's own organ accompaniment, made at the time of the first performance.

3. By and large, extracts from larger pieces have been omitted (though Hadley's anthem was simply too good to miss out, and may tempt choirs to programme the full cantata in a future concert).

Translations

Many, if not most, of the choirs using this book will never need to make use of the singing translations provided. Others—including, for example, those serving the largest Christian denomination in the United States—have little choice but to sing in English. It does not seem right that they and their listeners should be denied the experience of so much of the best English choral literature for lack of an English text. The policy in this volume, therefore, has been to provide singing translations for everything except the longest Latin pieces, such as Naylor's *Vox dicentis: Clama* and Tallis's *Loquebantur variis linguis*, which seem most likely to be performed either by concert choirs or in churches where the use of Latin is not an issue.

The principles governing the singing translations in the *Oxford Choral Classics* series are: to be as faithful as possible to the meaning and flavour of the originals; to alter the rhythms of the originals as little as possible; and to make the English texts as singable as possible. Where these principles come into conflict and one or more of them has to be sacrificed, singability remains the primary aim. The style of religious language is also a factor. Whilst respecting the viewpoint that religious texts should be presented in contemporary language, it seems appropriate that music of a past period should reflect the language of that time, especially when in most cases there is an extensive corpus of settings by that composer already in English that uses similarly 'historic' language. For those reasons, in the translations for this collection there has been no hesitation in using 'thou' or in echoing phrases from older bibles, hymns, and prayer books.

Editorial practice

The policy of the *Oxford Choral Classics* series is to use primary sources, printed or in manuscript, wherever possible, and this has resulted in the elimination of some long-standing errors. In presenting the editions, the aim is first and foremost to serve the practical needs of non-specialist choirs, keeping the music pages as clean and uncluttered as possible, though not neglecting the needs of the scholar. Prefatory staves are given for pre-1700 sources. References to clefs and pitch follow the standard conventions. Note values in early pieces have generally been reduced to give a ♩ pulse; pitches have been transposed to suit standard voice ranges; editorial barring has been shown in a modern, standard way; and key signatures have been modernized. Punctuation, capitalization, and spelling of texts has been modernized, with the *Liber Usualis* as a principal point of reference for Latin texts and the Authorized Version for biblical texts. Psalm numbering follows Protestant usage. Editorially completed text underlay is not shown in italics, as this convention would present a confusing appearance when italics are already being used for the singing translation. Indications of ligature and coloration are omitted, though care has been taken with editorial underlay never to move to a new syllable in the middle of a ligature. Obvious scribal or printing errors in sources are silently corrected; cases of doubt or discrepancy between sources are listed in the commentary. Dynamics and expression marks have been positioned as in their sources, even where this may lead to slightly differing policies across the volume. Some composers, for instance Wesley, are not always wholly consistent in their dynamic schemes, and editorial dynamics have been added only where considered really necessary. All material in square brackets or in small print is editorial. In pre-1700 pieces, full-size accidentals are those that appear in the source; they are silently omitted when made unnecessary by a modern key signature, and also omitted for immediate repetitions of the same note in the same bar. Small accidentals are editorial. Cautionary accidentals are shown full size in round brackets. Cancelling accidentals customary in modern notation but absent in the source are shown full size in round brackets. Crossed slurs are editorial; dotted slurs have been inserted only when felt to be really necessary, and indicate that the underlay of the translated text and the original text differ. Syllabic slurs in voice parts, as used in modern publishing style, have not generally been added. Beaming and stemming of notes has been modernized.

Not everyone will agree with the inclusion of editorial suggestions of tempo and dynamics. To some choir directors they are an irritation, whereas to others they are thoroughly useful. As a compromise solution, suggested dynamics have been added into the keyboard parts in pre-1700 pieces, making them available to those who would like to consider them but easy to ignore for those who would not. Such markings are, necessarily, a general guide only, and cannot take account of the natural rise and fall of individual voice parts within a polyphonic texture. So many factors—not least of all the size and acoustic of a building—can affect the choice of speed and dynamics between performances, even by the same choir on consecutive nights, that such editorial markings should be treated as tentative suggestions only, and never as a prescription. For that reason, dynamic suggestions have not generally been added to verse (solo) sections, as soloists will surely wish to follow their own interpretations.

Keyboard parts

Keyboard parts of *a cappella* pieces are given in their most readable and playable form, without always showing the movement of individual polyphonic voices, especially where these cross. This sometimes results in apparent parallel fifths and octaves, but this is surely preferable to the frequent sight of upstems and downstems crossed. Where all the voices of a texture are impossible to play, the keyboard reduction has been discreetly simplified. Editorial *musica ficta* is incorporated into the reduction without qualification, surely preferable to the alternative of a mass of small or bracketed accidentals (most of whose origins can in any case, if required, be quickly deduced from the vocal lines above). Accidentals follow the convention of homophonic keyboard music, not polyphony, and are not duplicated within a bar at the same pitch if in different voices.

Seventeenth- and eighteenth-century pieces originally published with a *basso continuo* part (even where this is no more than a *basso seguente*) have been assumed to be intended for accompanied performance. Those Restoration anthems by Purcell and his contemporaries that were undoubtedly accompanied by continuo instruments, but for which no continuo part survives, have had their figured basses editorially provided. Where relevant and apposite, any figures from the original figured bass have been included (though often in the original manuscripts these are written in a different, sometimes later, hand), with such existing figures editorially enhanced and completed to create a consistent style of figured bass across the volume. The wide variety of styles of 'shorthand' figures have also been standardized to meet modern editorial practice. Such editorial continuo realizations are intended both as a workable solution for performers who wish to play them exactly as written (when they will produce a thoroughly satisfactory continuo part), and also as a basis for more experienced players who may wish to create their own realizations from the figured bass alone.

Full scores and parts for instrumentally accompanied items are available on rental from the publisher or copyright owner (see Index of Orchestrations, p. 378).

Acknowledgements

My grateful thanks go to the many people without whom I could not have created this volume. Suggestions of works for inclusion came from, among others, Helen Hogh, Margaret King, Peter Nardone, John Scott, and Roger White. The generous assistance of the librarians of many notable collections across Britain is acknowledged, especially: the staff of the Rare Books and Manuscripts department of the British Library; Peter Horton at the Royal College of Music, London; Mark Statham of Gonville and Caius College, Cambridge; Frank Bowles at Cambridge University Library; Martin Holmes at the Bodleian Library, Oxford; and the staff and librarians of the Fitzwilliam Museum, Cambridge; the Victoria and Albert Museum, London; and Christ Church College, Oxford. Helpful advice on sources of texts and manuscripts was given by Andrew Carwood, Nick Flower, Peter Nardone, and Geoffrey Webber. John Morehen loaned a hard-to-find microfilm, and Lynda Sayce and John Harte expertly helped locate a significant number of original volumes and manuscripts. At OUP, David Blackwell, Head of Music Publishing, has given steadfast support throughout the production of the volume, and Anna Williams was invaluable in contacting librarians across Britain to gain access for me to copies of some remarkable manuscripts. My editor Robyn Elton has been a tower of strength in seeing through and co-ordinating a complex operation with patience, good humour, and an inspiring eye for detail. Great thanks are due to John Rutter for entrusting this important collection to me, for ensuring that the high standards of previous volumes in the series were maintained, for sharing innumerable insights, and for showing me a host of tricks in the Sibelius music setting programme that I would never have worked out for myself.

Greatest thanks, however, go to my wife Viola, who patiently tolerated my late nights and early mornings, my long, library-burrowing, absent hours, the piles of manuscripts taking up ever more space in our office, and the occasional exasperations and more frequent triumphs as another number was completed. Without her good-humoured support the volume would still be nowhere near completion. Our young son Johannes has watched the volume progress with great excitement, and nothing would give the project greater purpose and completion, and me greater pleasure, than if, in a few years' time, he himself should be singing from a copy of this volume. So it is to him that this volume is dedicated, as a representative of all those singers who hopefully for many years to come will continue that most noble of traditions: choirs across the world singing the finest English church music.

ROBERT KING
Suffolk, June 2010

1. Rejoice in the Lord alway

Philippians 4: 4–7

ANON.
(mid-16th century)

* Vocal parts reconstructed from surviving organ score. See commentary.

2. Jesu, the very thought of thee

Words attributed to
St Bernard of Clairvaux (12th century)
Translation by E. Caswall

EDWARD C. BAIRSTOW
(1874–1946)

3. Salvator mundi

(O Saviour of the world)

Book of Common Prayer
(Antiphon in the Office of the Visitation of the Sick)
English version by Robert King

JOHN BLOW
(c.1649–1708)

4. O where shall wisdom be found?

Job 28: 12–15, 18, 20–1, 23–8

WILLIAM BOYCE
(1711–79)

5. Ave verum Corpus

(Hail, O hail, true body)

Sequence Hymn for Corpus Christi
by Pope Innocent VI (d. 1362)
English version by Robert King

WILLIAM BYRD
*(c.*1540–1623*)*

Psalm 118: 24
English version by Robert King

6. Haec dies
(This is the great day)

WILLIAM BYRD
*(c.*1540–1623*)*

7. Justorum animae

(God holds the righteous)

Wisdom 3: 1–3
English version by Robert King

WILLIAM BYRD
(c.1540–1623)

8. Sing joyfully

Psalm 81: 1–4

WILLIAM BYRD
(c.1540–1623)

9. They are at rest

Words by John Henry Newman
(1801–90)

EDWARD ELGAR
(1857–1934)

10. O clap your hands

Psalm 47

ORLANDO GIBBONS
(1583–1625)

11. O Lord, in thy wrath

Psalm 6: 1–4

ORLANDO GIBBONS
(1583–1625)

SOPRANO 1: O Lord, in thy wrath, in thy wrath re-buke me

SOPRANO 2: O Lord, in thy wrath re-buke me

ALTO 1: O Lord, in thy wrath re-buke me not,

ALTO 2: O Lord, in thy wrath, O

TENOR: O Lord, in thy wrath

BASS: O Lord, in thy

Andante espressivo ♩ = 66

(for rehearsal only)

p

* Source gives ♮, presenting an unlikely, tritone-based harmony.

12. Lord, for thy tender mercy's sake

Words from Henry Bull:
Christian Prayers and Holy Meditations (1568)

RICHARD FARRANT
or JOHN HILTON
(late 16th century)

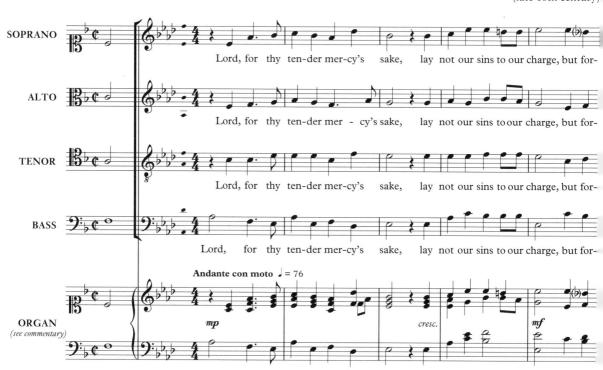

13. These are they which follow the Lamb

Revelation 14: 4–5

JOHN GOSS
(1800–80)

14. Lord, let me know mine end

Psalm 39: 4–7, 12–13

MAURICE GREENE
(1696–1755)

15. My song is love unknown

(from *Cantata for Lent*)

Words by Samuel Crossman (1623–83)
and Edward Denny (1796–1889)
Text compiled by Charles Cudworth (1908–77)

PATRICK HADLEY
(1899–1973)

* Hadley also scored this anthem for orchestra. Score and parts are available on rental (see p. 378).

But O,— my Friend,— my Friend in-deed, Who at my need his life did spend.

(Man.)

Più mosso

In life no house, no home My Lord on earth might have; In death no friend-ly

mf

mf

rit. **Tempo primo** ♩ = 60

tomb— But what a stran - ger gave. What— may I say? Heaven was his home;

p

[Ped.]

rit.

But mine the tomb where-in he lay.

-rise, and with thy morn - ing beams Chase all our_ griefs a - way.___ Come, bless - ed_

Lord, bid_ ev - 'ry shore And an - sw'ring is - land sing___ The prai - ses_

of_ thy_ roy - al Name And_ own_ thee_ as___ their King.___ Bid

ee commentary (bar 83)

16. Faire is the heaven

Words by Edmund Spenser
(1553–99)

WILLIAM H. HARRIS
(1883–1973)

17. O how glorious is the kingdom

Antiphon for the
Feast of All Saints

BASIL HARWOOD
(1859–1949)

18. Like as the hart desireth the waterbrooks

Psalm 42: 1–3

HERBERT HOWELLS
(1892–1983)

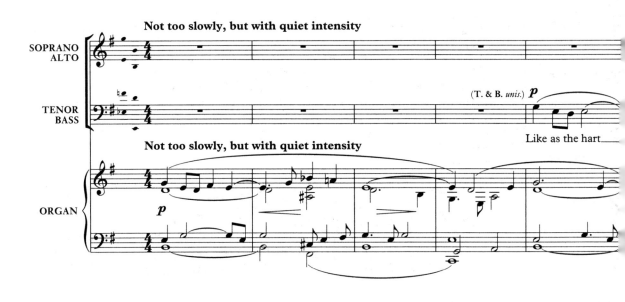

19. Greater love hath no man

Words from the Bible
(*see commentary*)

JOHN IRELAND
(1879–1962)

* Ireland also scored this anthem for orchestra. Scores and parts are available on rental (see p. 378).

20. The souls of the righteous

Wisdom 3: 1–3

GERAINT LEWIS
(b.1958)

21. Hear my prayer

Psalm 55: 2–8, paraphrased by
William Bartholomew (1793–1867)

FELIX MENDELSSOHN
(1809–47)

* Mendelssohn also scored this anthem for orchestra. Score and parts are available on rental (see p. 378).

---

* The intention of the apparently conflicting pauses seems to be for the organ to hold the ♩. for the written length under the soloist's paused 'God', and the organ then to lift the chord while the soloist completes the paused note, singing the last three syllables unaccompanied.

Con un poco più di moto

22. Nolo mortem peccatoris

(I ask not the death of sinners)

Poem probably by John Redford (d. 1547)
Translation by Robert King

THOMAS MORLEY
(c.1557/8–1602)

23. Vox dicentis: Clama

Isaiah 40: 6–11

E. W. NAYLOR
(1867–1934)

The voice said: Cry;   *And he said: What shall I cry?*

All flesh is grass, and all the goodliness thereof is as the flower of the field

Surely the people is grass

The grass withereth, the flower fadeth.

But the word of our God shall stand for ever.

O Zion, that bringest good tidings, get thee up into the high mountain;

lift up thy voice with strength;

Behold your God!

Behold, the Lord God will come with strong hand,

and his arm shall rule for him: *behold, his reward is with him, and his work before him.*

He shall feed his flock like a shepherd: he shall gather the lambs with his arm, and carry them in his bosom, and shall gently lead those that are with young.

24. Ave Maria
(*Honour we Mary*)

after Luke 1: 28, 42
English version by Robert King

ROBERT PARSONS
(*c*.1535–71/2)

25. Ascendit Deus
(God has ascended)

Psalms 47: 5, 103: 19
English version by Robert King

PETER PHILIPS
(c.1560/1–1628)

26. Hear my prayer, O Lord

Psalm 102: 1

HENRY PURCELL
(1659–95)

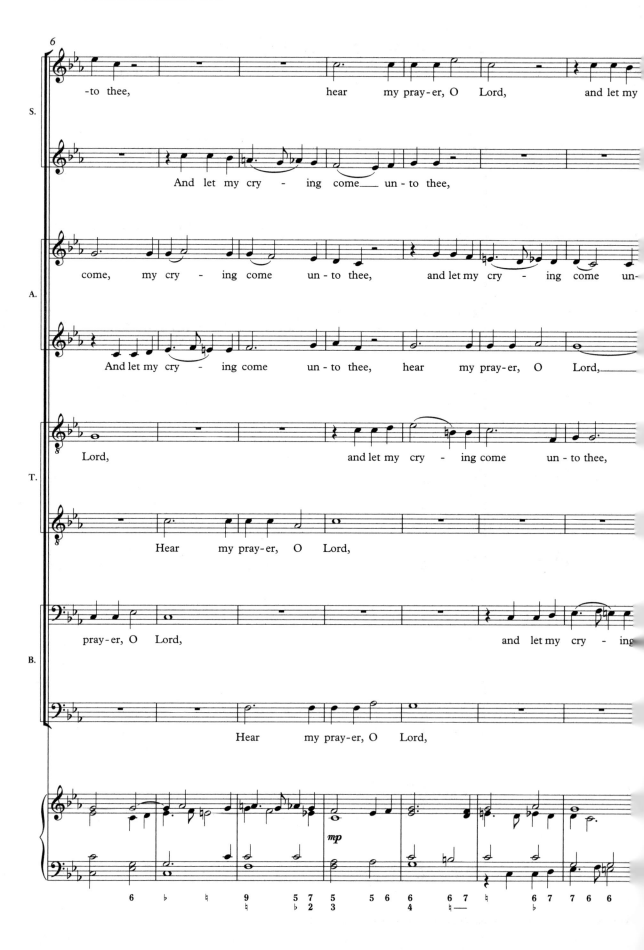

27. I was glad when they said unto me

Psalm 122: 1, 4–7

HENRY PURCELL
(1659–95)

28. Let mine eyes run down with tears

Jeremiah 14: 17–22

HENRY PURCELL
(1659–95)

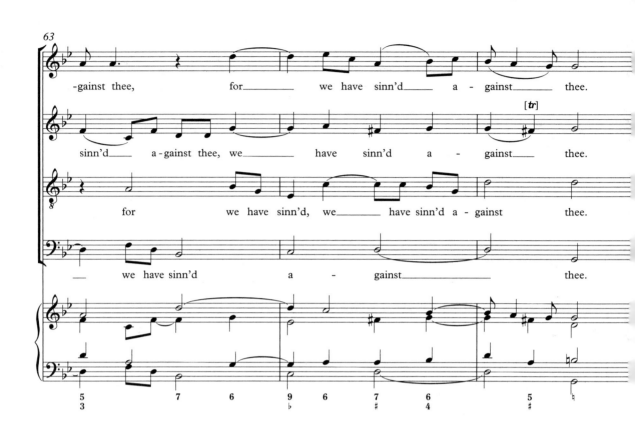

29. Lord, how long wilt thou be angry?

Psalm 79: 5, 8–9, 13

HENRY PURCELL
(1659–

30. Remember not, Lord, our offences

Words from the Litany

HENRY PURCELL
(1659–95)

31. God so loved the world
(from *The Crucifixion*)

John 3: 16–17

JOHN STAINER
(1840–1901)

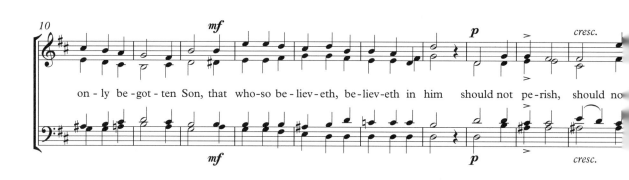

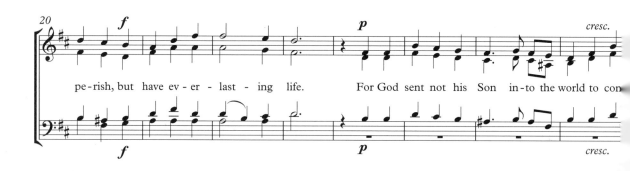

him might be sav - ed. God so loved the world,___ God so loved the

world,___ that he gave his on - ly be - got - ten Son, that who-so be - liev-eth, be-

world, that he

-liev-eth in him should not pe -rish, should not pe -rish, but have ev - er - last - ing

life, ev - er - last - ing life, ev - er - last - ing, ev - er - last - ing life.

ev - er - last - ing life.

God so loved the world,___ God so loved the world,___ God so loved the world.

32. I saw the Lord

Isaiah 6: 1–4
and anonymous 11th-century Latin hymn
translated by J. D. Chambers (1803–93)

JOHN STAINER
(1840–1901)

[Man.]

VERSE

40

wor - ship thee, And with the songs that an-gels sing U - nite the hymns of praise we bring.

wor - ship thee, And with the songs that an-gels sing U - nite the hymns of praise we bring.

wor - ship thee, And with the songs that an-gels sing U - nite the hymns of praise__ we bring. O

wor - ship thee, And with the songs that an-gels sing U - nite the hymns of praise we bring.

CHOIRS I & II

The whole earth is full of his

The whole earth is full of his

The whole earth is full of his

The whole earth is full of his

33. Beati quorum via

(How blessed are faithful souls)

Psalm 119: 1
English version by Robert King

CHARLES VILLIERS STANFORD
(1852–1924)

34. Coelos ascendit hodie

(Heaven receives our Lord today)

Words: Medieval Ascension hymn
English version by Robert King

CHARLES VILLIERS STANFORD
(1852–1924)

35. How beauteous are their feet

Words by Isaac Watts
(1674–1748)

CHARLES VILLIERS STANFORD
(1852–1924)

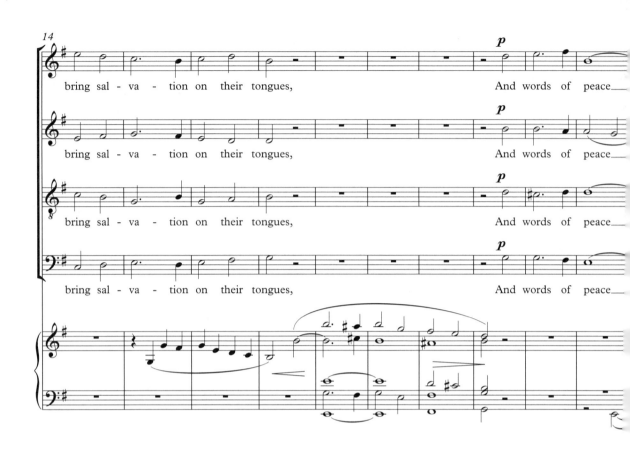

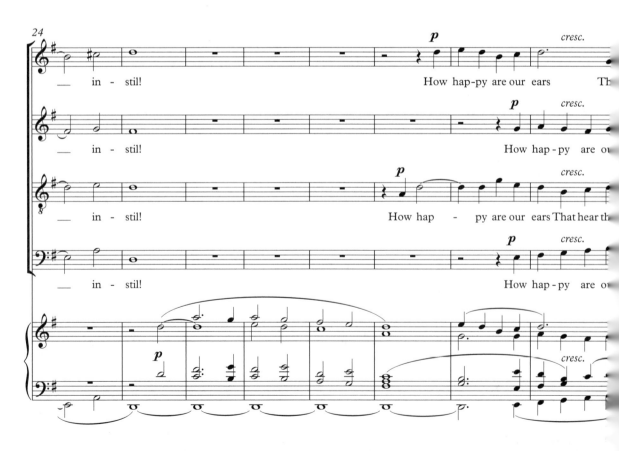

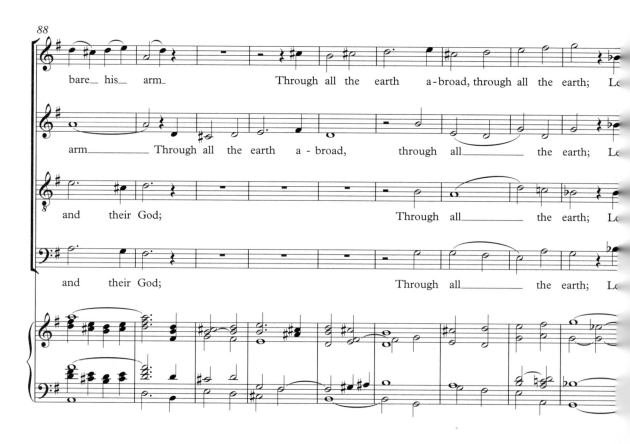

36. I heard a voice from heaven

Revelation 14: 13

CHARLES VILLIERS STANFORD
(1852–1924)

fol - - low them, their_ works_ fol - low them._

fol - - low them,_ their works fol - low them._

- low them,_ their_ works_ fol - low them._

fol - low them, their_ works fol - low them._

Più lento

Bless - ed, bless - ed, bless - ed are_ the dead which

Bless - ed, bless - ed, bless - ed are_ the dead which

Bless - ed bless - ed, bless - ed are_ the dead_ which

Bless - ed, bless - ed, bless - ed are the dead which

Più lento

hoir directors may prefer to have the soprano soloist sing the upper line and the tutti sopranos the lower line.

37. Justorum animae
(The hand of God holds faithful souls)

Wisdom 3: 1–3
English version by Robert King

CHARLES VILLIERS STANFORD
(1852–1924)

38. Loquebantur variis linguis

arum Responsory for
First Vespers at Pentecost

THOMAS TALLIS
(*c.1505–85*)

The apostles spoke in many tongues: alleluia.

Of the great works of God: alleluia.

al - le-lu - - - ia, al - le-lu - - ia.

- - ia, al - le-lu - ia, al - le - lu - - ia.

- - - - - ia, al - le-lu - - ia.

- - ia, al - le-lu - - ia, al - le-lu - - ia.

- - ia._____

-ia, al - le-lu - - ia, al - le-lu - ia.

- le-lu - - - ia, al - le - lu - ia.

Re - ple - - ti sunt om - nes Spi - ri - tu__ San - - cto,__

They were all filled with the Holy Spirit

et ce - - - - pe - runt_____ lo - - qui.__

and began to speak in many tongues.

Of the great works of God: alleluia.

39. O Lord, give thy Holy Spirit

idley's Prayers, 1566

THOMAS TALLIS
(*c.*1505–85)

40. O nata lux de lumine
(*O holy light once born of light*)

Office Hymn for Lauds on
the Feast of the Transfiguration
English version by Robert King

THOMAS TALLI
(*c.*1505–8

41. If ye love me

John 14: 15–17

THOMAS TALLIS
(c.1505–8...)

42. Dum transisset Sabbatum

Mark 16: 1–2

JOHN TAVERNER
(c.1490–154)

When the sabbath was past Mary Magdalene, and Mary the mother of James, and Salome had brought sweet spices

that they might come and anoint Jesus.

And early in the morning on the first day of the week they came unto the sepulchre at the rising of the sun.

That they might come and anoint Jesus.

Glory be to the Father, and to the Son, and to the Holy Spirit.

43. When David heard

Samuel 18: 33

THOMAS TOMKINS
(1572–1656)

44. O how amiable are thy dwellings

Psalms 84: 1–4; 90: 17 and paraphrase of
Psalm 90:1 by Isaac Watts (1674–1748)

RALPH VAUGHAN WILLIAMS
(1872–1958)

* This anthem is also available in arrangements for brass and for strings. Scores and parts are available (see p. 378).

45. O taste and see

Psalm 34: 8

RALPH VAUGHAN WILLIAMS
(1872–1958)

The first edition notes that this motet may also be sung in the key of G flat.

46. Set me as a seal upon thine heart

Adapted from the
Song of Solomon 8: 6–7

WILLIAM WALTON
(1902–83)

47. Blessed be the God and Father

I Peter 1: 3–5, 15, 17, 22–5

SAMUEL SEBASTIAN WESLEY
(1810–7...)

lively hope by the resurrection of Jesus Christ from the dead,

lively hope by the resurrection of Jesus Christ from the dead,

lively hope by the resurrection of Jesus Christ from the dead,

lively hope by the resurrection of Jesus Christ from the dead,

Gt. Diaps, Sw. coupled

L'istesso tempo

ALTO*, TENOR & BASS

[*mf*]

To an in-he-rit-ance in-cor-rupt-i-ble and un-de-fi-led, that fad-eth not a-

[*mf*]

Gt. Open Diap, Sw. uncoupled

Ped.

cresc.

-way, re-serv-ed in heaven for you, who are kept by the pow-er of God, through faith un-to sal-

[*cresc.*]

esley's intention was for his (male) altos to sing here in bass voice. In mixed choir performances, female altos tacent.
ernatively, this passage and bars 107–17 may be sung by a solo bass.

-va - tion, rea-dy to be re-veal-ed in the last time.

SOPRANO SOLO (Dec.)*

But as he which hath call-ed you is ho - ly, so be_ ye

ho-ly in all man-ner of__ con - ver - sa-tion. Pass the time of your so-journ-ing here in

fear,____ in__ fear.__

*Decani: in English cathedrals this is the half of the choir which stands at the conductor's right, in the south choir stalls.

Moderato ♩ = 104

SOLO (Dec.)

Love one an-o-ther with a pure heart fer-vent-ly, See that ye

love one an-o-ther, Love one an-o-ther with a pure heart

fer-vent-ly, See that ye love one an-o-ther, Love one an-

-o-ther with a pure heart fer-vent-ly, a pure

heart fer-vent-ly, See that ye love one an-o-ther,

God. For all flesh is as grass, and all the glo - ry of man as the flow - er of grass. The

grass wi - ther - eth, and the flow - er____ there - of fall - eth a way.

Clarabella

Sw. Reed

f Full Org.

Allegretto ♩ = 100

ff

But the word of the Lord en - dur - eth for ev - er,

ff

But the word of the Lord en - dur - eth for ev - er,

ff

But the word of the Lord en - dur - eth for ev - er,

ff

But the word of the Lord en - dur - eth for ev - er,

Allegretto ♩ = 100

(voices alone)

ff Full Org.

Ped.

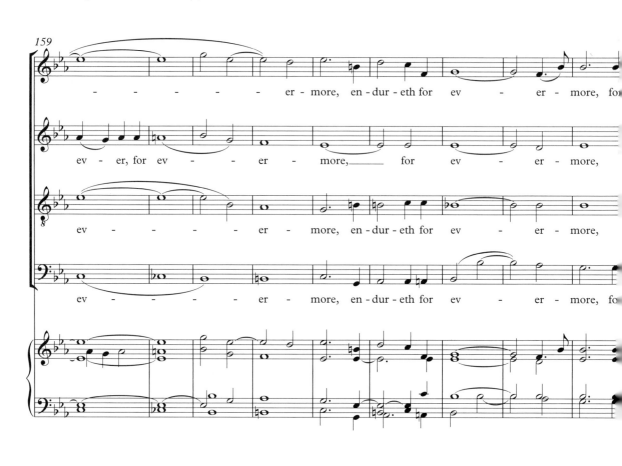

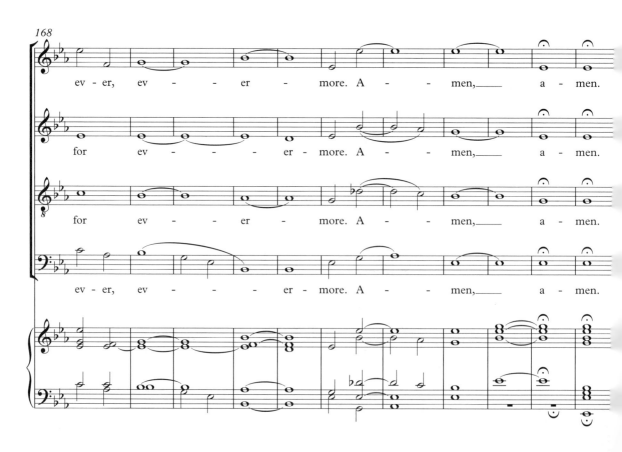

48. Praise the Lord, O my soul

Psalms 103: 1; 3: 5; 5: 2–3, 12*, 7–8; 4: 8

SAMUEL SEBASTIAN WESLEY
(1810–76)

The Authorised Version of the Bible numbers this as verse 11, but Wesley set from the Book of Common Prayer, where it is verse 12.

give ear, O Lord, give ear un-to my pray'r, give_ ear_____ un-to my pray'r.

*TUTTI **p***

My

TUTTI **p**

My

TUTTI **p**

My

voice shalt thou hear, ear-ly in the morn-ing will I di - rect my_ pray'r, give

voice shalt thou hear be-times, O Lord,__ ear-ly in the morn-ing will I di-rect my_ pray'r to thee, give

voice shalt thou hear be-times, O Lord,__ ear-ly in the morn-ing will I di-rect my pray'r to

Wesley's intention was for his (male) altos to sing here in bass voice. In choirs without male altos, directors may wish to allocate
ors to sing the alto line from bars 108–20.

* Choir directors may wish to allocate tenors or even basses to sing the alto line from bars 177–85.

Introduction only played if 'Lead me Lord' is performed separately.

Lead me, Lord, lead me in thy right-eous-ness, make thy way plain be-fore my face. Lead me, Lord, Lord,

Lead me, Lord,

Lead me, Lord,

Lead me, Lord,

lead me in thy right-eous-ness, make thy way plain be-fore my face. For it is thou, Lord,

lead me in thy right-eous-ness, make thy way plain be-fore my face.

lead me in thy right-eous-ness, make thy way plain be-fore my face.

lead me in thy right-eous-ness, make thy way plain be-fore my face.

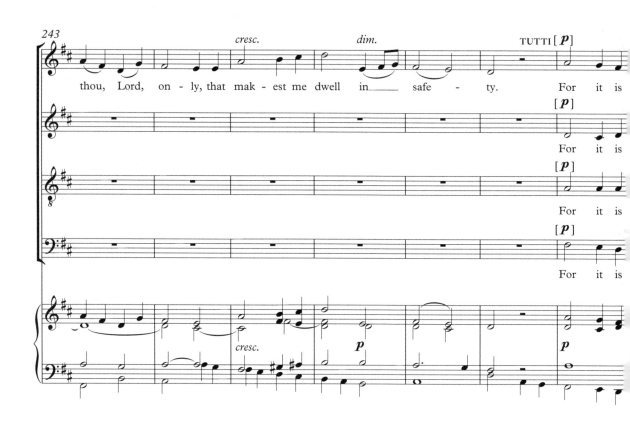

49. Thou wilt keep him in perfect peace

Isaiah 26: 3; Psalm 139: 12; I John 1: 5;
Psalm 119: 175 and the Lord's Prayer

SAMUEL SEBASTIAN WESLEY
(1810–76)

50. Wash me throughly

Psalm 51: 2–3

SAMUEL SEBASTIAN WESLEY
(1810–76)

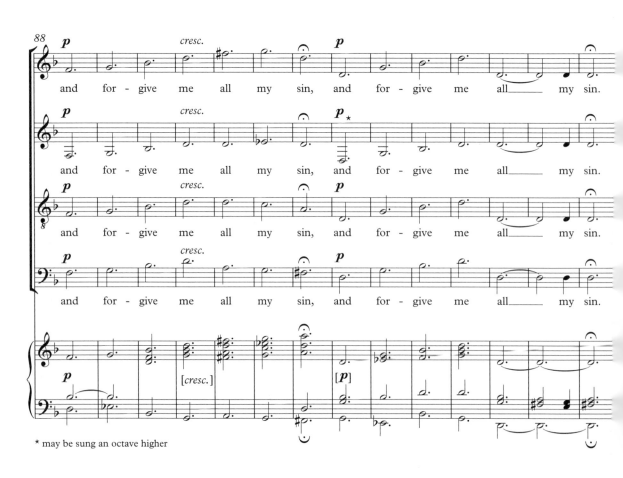

* may be sung an octave higher

51. O thou the central orb

Words by H. R. Bramley
(1833–1917)

CHARLES WOOD
(1866–1926)

COMMENTARY

Notes

1. Psalms are numbered according to Protestant usage.
2. Specific references to musical notes in the scores are given thus: bar number (Arabic), stave number counting down from t stave in each system (Roman), symbol number in the bar (Arabic). For example, in *Rejoice in the Lord alway*, 9 iv 5 ref to the last note in the bass part of b. 9.
3. Pitch and rhythmic references are given in terms of the editions in this book, not in terms of the original sources. Wh editions are transposed and note values shortened, so are all references to variants.

1. Anon.: *Rejoice in the Lord alway*

This short anthem appears in the Mulliner Book, an important Tudor collection of keyboard pieces compiled around the 1560s by Thomas Mulliner, who was known to have been *modulator organorum* (organist) of Corpus Christi College, Oxford, in 1563. Among the 121 pieces contained in the volume is a keyboard transcription of an anthem for four voices, with its main body of text (from the Authorized Version of the Bible) added in a later hand. This text gives little indication as to exact underlay, which has here been revised to fit the original keyboard score more closely than in some other modern editions. The rhythm of the music indicates that the original text would have been that from the 1549 Prayer Book (where this text provides the Epistle for the Fourth Sunday in Advent), rather than that written in the manuscript, which does not fit the original rhythms.

Source: BL Add. MS 30513, *Mulliner Book. Variants:* 11 ii 1–2: editorial / 11 iii 2: corrected from *e* to *d* to avoid parallel fifths with S; also mirrored in the organ / 14 iii 3 & 14 iv 2: ♩ changed to ♪♪ to match S / 16 ii 2: *g* in source / 17 iii 4–18 iii 2: source shows ♩ ♩ / 48 iv 3 & 49 iii 1: ♩ altered to ♩. ♪ to match A. *Method:* All placing of text is editorial. The organ part is printed as in the source. A few slight rhythmic adaptations have been necessarily made in the vocal parts to fit the text; these can be gleaned by comparison of the voice parts with the organ part and thus are not here additionally noted.

2. Bairstow: *Jesu, the very thought of thee*

The Huddersfield-born Edward Cuthbert Bairstow studied organ with John Farmer at Balliol College, Oxford. He received further tuition from Walter Alcock, and also studied at Durham University, where he received a Bachelor of Music degree in 1894, a doctorate in 1901, and was eventually appointed professor in 1929. He was organist of York Minster from 1913 until his death in 1946, when he was succeeded by his former pupil Francis Jackson. He was knighted in 1932. A notoriously terse man, Bairstow refused an offer to succeed Frederick Bridge at Westminster Abbey, preferring to remain in his home county of Yorkshire, where he enjoyed a considerable reputation as a conductor of choral societies. Instead he recommended his erstwhile pupil Ernest Bullock, who was duly appointed to the post. His bluff exterior hid a sensitive musicality, as this well-crafted anthem admirably demonstrates.

Source: First edition (OUP, 1925).

3. Blow: *Salvator mundi (O Saviour of the world)*

John Blow's influence and importance in the rich seam of Restoration composers has usually been overshadowed by the genius of Purcell, and his music has accordingly not achie the status that it has perhaps deserved. Holding positions both the Chapel Royal and Westminster Abbey, he wa prolific composer for the church, and the best of his anthe both those with strings and those for choir alone, stand well in comparison to those of his illustrious but short-li colleague. *Salvator mundi*, a setting of the antiphon in Office of the Visitation of the Sick, and one of the sm handful of Blow's works to be written in Latin, shows expressive, Italianate use of dissonance, as well as a fine se of small-scale musical architecture.

Source: Christ Church College, Oxford, Mus. MS *Variants:* Continuo figuring and realization is editorial. 5♦ 5: ♩. altered to ♩ ♩ / 51 iv 2–3: slur removed to enable ♦ underlay.

4. Boyce: *O where shall wisdom be found?*

William Boyce is widely regarded as the leading English-b composer of the late Baroque, writing for both the chu and the stage. He was a chorister at St Paul's Cathedral a after his voice changed, became a pupil of the cathed organist, Maurice Greene. Although appointed organist c Michael's, Cornhill, in 1736, he did not move further into world of cathedral organists, but instead concentrated composition. In 1736 he was appointed Composer to Chapel Royal and wrote for that establishment a substa number of anthems, while also enjoying much success in theatre and the opera house. After the death of Green 1755 he was appointed Master of the King's Musick. deafness gradually overtook him he turned increasingl what would nowadays be called musicology. His substan three-volume *Cathedral Music* is a unique and impor survey of church music that had been in the repertoire the last two hundred years. At Boyce's death, Charles We wrote: 'A more modest man than Dr Boyce I have never kn I have never heard him speak a vain or ill-natured word, ei to exalt himself or deprecate another'. That gentility of chara comes across in this delightful five-part verse anth elegantly crafted and showing fine technical command.

Source: BL 'Royal Manuscript' RM 27. *Method:* The organ interludes (bb. 1–4, 18–19, 30–2, 62–5, 82–4, 10 125–6, 138–9) are original. Elsewhere the original o book is partly figured, though some figures appear to be ' additions; the figures have been completed editorially, as the realization. *Variants:* 93 i 2: source erroneously gives

5. Byrd: *Ave verum Corpus (Hail, O hail, true body)*

William Byrd's two-volume *Gradualia*, first publishe 1605 and 1607, and subsequently reprinted in 1610, substantial publication in five partbooks that offers

der no fewer than 32 numbers set for five voices, 20 for
ur voices, and 11 for three voices. The collection contains
o cycles of motets, as well as a number of miscellaneous
ms that fall outside the liturgical scheme of the main body
 the set. Dedicated to two members of the Catholic
bility, the first Earl of Northampton, Henry Howard, and
rd's own patron Sir John Petre, such a collection of
tholic polyphony surely must have reflected raised hopes
t the recusant community would enjoy an easier life under
 new King James I.

Source: William Byrd, *Gradualia ac cantiones sacrae,*
inis, quaternis, trinisque vocibus concinnatae. Lib. primus
ndon, 1610), BL K.2.F.7. *Variants:* 19–20 i–iv: source
nts 'unde' rather than 'unda' / 42 iii 1–2: first syllable
rred across ♩♪ in source / 43: source writes out repeated
tion in full.

Byrd: *Haec dies (This is the great day)*

irty-seven of Byrd's motets were published in the two
umes of *Cantiones sacrae*, published in 1589 and 1591.
dicated to the Earl of Worcester and Baron Lumley, they
y have been intended by Byrd to help re-establish himself
court after a decade during which his star had been
ning. *Haec dies* is a forward-looking setting that reflects
 growing popularity of the madrigal in its vivid
rd-painting.
Source: Cantiones Sacrae, Liber Secundus (1591), BL
.f.5. *Method:* Original note values retained in duple-time
ions; in triple-time sections note values have been halved.

Byrd: *Justorum animae (God holds the righteous)*

other setting from the *Gradualia*, *Justorum animae* is the
ultimate of the 32 five-part settings. The typography is
utifully clear, leaving little doubt as to underlay or *musica
a*. With the motet being largely homophonic, the setting of
 last word in the Offertory for All Saints' Day, 'pace'
ace'), is made all the more effective by its use of melisma.
*Source: Gradualia ac Cantiones Sacrae, quinis, quaternis,
isque vocibus concinnatae. Lib primus* (London, 1610),
RM.15.d.1. *Variants:* 'Justorum' was spelt 'Iustorum' in
source.

Byrd: *Sing joyfully*

s jubilant, six-part setting is evidently a late work, similar
tyle to the English motets contained in Byrd's collection
611, *Psalms, Songs and Sonnets*. The source is a matched
 of manuscript partbooks created by Thomas Myriell
580–1625). Myriell was a clergyman by profession, but
est remembered as an assiduous and prolific collector
music editions, thanks to his remarkable collation of 229
ems, madrigals, and motets by various late sixteenth-
 early seventeenth-century composers: *Tristitiae
edium*. Dated on its engraved title page as 1616—though
 year has been questioned by some scholars—the part-
ks are now preserved in the British Library.
*ource: Tristitiae Remedium. Cantiones selectissimae,
rsorum tum autorum...*, BL Add. MSS 29372–7 (voice
s); Durham Cathedral Library MS A1 (organ part).
hod: The organ part incorporates that contained in the
ham source but has been filled out editorially with other
al lines without comment. *Variants:* 48 v 2: 'ev'n'
ected to 'and' to match text in other voices.

9. Elgar: *They are at rest*

For a composer who wrote so extensively for choir, Elgar
composed surprisingly little for the church. As a Roman
Catholic living in an English musical world that was heavily
dominated by Anglican composers and organists, he may
have felt himself in matters religious to be something of an
outsider. Commissioned by Sir Walter Parratt to write an
anthem to be sung on the anniversary of Queen Victoria's
death, Elgar turned for his libretto once again to the writings
of Cardinal Newman (1801–90), who had provided the text
for his *The Dream of Gerontius* (1900). Newman's poem,
part of his *Lyra Apostolica*, is an evocation of the souls of the
blessed at rest in paradise, surrounded and protected by an
angelic host. Elgar's 'Elegy for unaccompanied chorus' was
first performed at the Royal Mausoleum at Frogmore on 22
January 1910.
Source: First edition (Novello, 1910). *Variants:* double
bars at b. 3 & b. 13 removed. The original piano part, with
its sometimes slightly idiosyncratic expression marks, has
been retained.

10. Gibbons: *O clap your hands*

This substantial eight-part anthem was performed on 17 May
1622 when Orlando Gibbons and his friend William Heyther
were both admitted to the degree of Doctor of Music at
Oxford University. Gibbons was born in Oxford and sang in
the choir of King's College, Cambridge, where his older
brother Edward was Master of the Choristers. After taking
his degree at Cambridge he became first a Gentleman of the
Chapel Royal and then, in 1615, organist; one of his later
junior organists was Thomas Tomkins. In 1623 he was also
appointed organist of Westminster Abbey. Clearly a fine
player, he was described in one report as possessing 'the best
finger of the age'. His sudden death at Canterbury in 1625,
while awaiting the arrival of King Charles I's new bride,
Henrietta Maria, was surprising enough to cause a detailed
autopsy to be carried out: initial concerns that the cause had
been the plague were replaced by a diagnosis of apoplexy.

The source of this anthem, the 'Gostling' partbooks, notes
that the anthem was 'Dr Heather's Commencement Song
composed by Mr Orlan. Gibbons'. Heyther, a singer who is
buried in Westminster Abbey, founded a lectureship in music
at Oxford, and the university's chair of music is named after
him. Gibbons surely intended to impress both Heyther and
the assembled company with a demonstration of his skill at
handling an eight-part vocal texture. The 'Gostling' partbooks date from around 1675 and are a major record of
English sacred music both pre- and post-Civil War in their
documentation of works that were presumably being
performed during the Restoration in English cathedrals.
Gostling was a busy man, and not just because of his
exceptional singing voice, which led Purcell to write some of
his most famed bass solos. Besides holding a position as
Gentleman of the Chapel Royal, Gostling was also a Minor
Canon at both Canterbury Cathedral and St Paul's Cathedral,
and held two additional posts in parishes in Kent. In between
this work he was a collector and copier of music, acquiring
and adding to a set of copies created by the singer and
copyist Stephen Bing (d. 1681); those copies formed the basis
for his set.

For *O clap your hands*, a single, earlier partbook also
survives (BM Add. MS 29289), containing only the second

alto line. Thought to date from around 1630, it may have been used at St Paul's Cathedral and contains several significant discrepancies in underlay with the 'Gostling' books. However, it seems more consistent to take the entire setting from a unified set of partbooks, rather than use seven books from Gostling and add to them one solitary line from a different copyist.

Source: York Minster Library, 'Gostling' partbooks, MSS M.1/1–1/8. *Variants:* 59 viii 4–60 viii 2: underlay editorial / 83 vi 2: source gives erroneous *e* / 128 iii 5: source gives both *a♭* and *f*, the latter note presumably an error.

11. Gibbons: *O Lord, in thy wrath*
As well as being an exceptional keyboard player, Gibbons was also a fine and melodious composer, particularly of vocal music. His masterful, six-part setting of the mournful text of Psalm 6 is preserved in a set of partbooks thought to have been compiled around 1625–35 by John Barnard, a Minor Canon of St Paul's Cathedral. The manuscript is accurate, with the underlay especially clearly indicated. No organ part survives.

Source: Royal College of Music, MSS 1045–51. *Variants:* 27: some books erroneously write 'heare' instead of 'heale'.

12. Farrant or Hilton: *Lord, for thy tender mercy's sake*
Uncertainty surrounds the authorship of this anthem. Of six manuscript sources, two attribute the piece to 'Farrant' and four to a 'John Hilton', but none are contemporary, all dating from after the deaths of both Richard Farrant and John Hilton the elder. Richard Farrant (*c.*1525/30–80) was a composer, choirmaster, playwright, and theatrical producer, who eventually simultaneously held positions as Master of the Children of the Chapel Royal and Master of the Choristers at St George's Chapel, Windsor. John Hilton the elder (d. *c.*1609) was a singer at Lincoln Cathedral before taking a position as organist at Trinity College, Cambridge. The available manuscript sources date from between 1645 and 1708; the two ascribing the work to Farrant do not contain the final 'Amen'. For this edition, the lower three parts have been taken from the earliest, Christ Church, manuscript, with the soprano part being reconstructed from a slightly later organ part in the same library. The closing 'Amen', quite probably not original, comes from an eighteenth-century copy held in the British Library.

Sources: A: Christ Church MSS 1220–4 (*c.*1645) for ATB vocal parts. B: Christ Church MS 437 (*c.*1670) for organ part (contains outer parts only). C: BL Harl. MS 7340 (dated 1707) used for the final 'Amen'. A & B ascribe the anthem to Richard Farrant whereas C ascribes it to 'Mr John Hilton'. *Method:* Soprano editorially reconstructed from organ part B with underlay based on the existing three vocal parts. Organ part taken from B with the inner parts editorially reconstructed from the alto and tenor parts. *Variants:* 21: the repeated section is written out in full / 22: 'Amen' in source C only. (The many slight divergences between sources A and C are not here noted.)

13. Goss: *These are they which follow the Lamb*
In 1838, having been organist of St Luke's Church, Chelsea, John Goss succeeded his former teacher Thomas Attwood as organist of St Paul's Cathedral, where he remained until his retirement in 1872, when his post was taken by his former

chorister, John Stainer. Much admired as a melodic composer who wrote especially well for voices, he w additionally appointed Composer to Her Majesty's Chap Royal in 1856. His 'Full anthem for the Feast of the H Innocents' was written in 1859.

Source: Novello (London, 1864), held at BL, H.1165.a.(*Method:* Original time signature ¢. Note values halv Organ part as originally printed. Editorial dynamics have b added in small type to the handful of original indications.

14. Greene: *Lord, let me know mine end*
Maurice Greene came from a well-to-do family and thought to have received his earliest music training a chorister at St Paul's Cathedral, where his first choirmas would have been Jeremiah Clarke. Having held vario London church organist posts, he was appointed organist St Paul's at the age of just 22. He knew—and later fell with—Handel, his pupils included Stanley and Boyce, and successively became Organist and Composer of the Cha Royal, Professor of Music at Cambridge, and Master of King's Musick. Not yet even aged 40, he held most ma musical appointments in the country, and then he turned publishing. Of his publications, the most important is F Select Anthems (1743), which provides an excellent survey his sacred compositions over the last 24 years. Included this collection is *Lord, let me know mine end*, and the c now preserved in the British Library appears to have b Greene's own copy, with its title page showing it pass through a number of distinguished owners, including Will Boyce, Dr Samuel Arnold (early editor of Handel's wor and Vincent Novello. Another, probably earlier, sourc signed 'Mr Green', suggesting that this may date from bef he received his doctorate in 1730, and this has been use the main source. However, the printed edition is fully figu and it is these figures that have been reproduced.

Source: BL Add. MS 17850. Also consulted, and so for figured bass: *Forty Select Anthems in Score... By Maurice Greene*, BL RM 14.d.19 (1743). *Method:* Mod conventions for figured bass have been incorporated, nota horizontal lines to indicate continuation of harmony ov changing bass note, rather than the publisher Wal separate figures; figures unnecessary for modern perform have been silently removed. The realization is edito Spelling and punctuation have been modernized. *Variants* ii 4: parallel fifths between S & A generated by pas seventh have been retained and repeated in organ / 65 appoggiatura present in RM 14 incorporated / 107 vi 2 error replaced with 5♭ / 112 vi 1–2: A minor figuring from 17850 preferred / 127: Greene marks final phrase *soft*.

15. Hadley: *My song is love unknown*
After active service in France in the First World War, Pat Hadley studied music at Pembroke College, Cambridge, afterwards composition with Vaughan Williams at the R College of Music (where he also studied conducting Adrian Boult). From 1925 Hadley taught at the RCM, in 1938 became a fellow of Gonville and Caius Coll Cambridge, and a lecturer in music; he was appoi Professor of Music in 1946. Influenced not only by song (to which Vaughan Williams had opened his eyes), by the landscapes of Ireland and Norfolk (to where retired in 1962), his music mixes a sense of introspection

netimes austerity with an often powerful atmospheric
esence.

The *Cantata for Lent* was first performed in a version for
orchestra on 5 April 1963 in Carlisle Cathedral as part of
St Bees Festival, and then in Manchester Cathedral on 8
ril with an organ accompaniment he had himself prepared.
dley had at first titled the work 'Lenten Meditation', and
bound orchestral score even bears that title, suggesting
t the name change was made late on during the
ceedings. The words were written and adapted during
52 by the Cambridge scholar and librarian Charles
dworth (1908–77), with those of the final section, *My
g is love unknown* (which forms the conclusion to Part II),
en from a hymn by the Suffolk-born, Cambridge-educated
nn writer Samuel Crossman (1623–83), and those for the
cluding chorale from what is probably the best-known
nn written by Sir Edward Denny (1796–1889). Hadley's
onse to this fine text is a splendid work, whose final
tion produces a lyrical, at times passionate tenor solo and
mpelling concluding chorale. Hadley had lost a leg in the
, and perhaps his inability to play the organ resulted in his
hestral reduction (which would work perfectly on the
no) requiring minor adjustment for today's organists,
ch this first printed edition makes.

ource: *Cantata for Lent*, Fitzwilliam Museum,
mbridge, MU. MSS 930 & 931. Also consulted: MU. MSS
(orchestral score), 997, & 998 (sketches). *Variants:* 9 i 1:
930 pencilled 'lovely' inked over to 'lovelier'; remains
ely' in MS 931 but 'lovelier' in MS 932. Latter option
n / 13 iii: *c♮* inserted / 14 iii 1–2, 15 iii 1–2, &
ii 1: pedal notes raised octave / 15 iii 1–2: raised octave /
9: accompaniment rescored / 29: organ diminuendo
ed / 30: speed and metronome mark added from full score
: in MS 932 organ plays the downbeat chord, missing in
& 931 / 93–9 & 109–14: organ part transposed down
ve with minor rewriting / 115–21: organ pedal part raised
ve / 121: organ last chord re-spaced.

Harris: *Faire is the heaven*

iam Harris won an organ scholarship to the Royal
ege of Music aged 16, and was soon made assistant at the
ple Church, London, moving on to hold the same
tion at Lichfield Cathedral. In 1919 he succeeded Hugh
n at New College, Oxford; in 1923 became Professor of
an and Composition at the RCM; and in 1933 was
ointed Organist at Christ Church, Oxford, before finally
ing to St George's Chapel, Windsor, where he was to
in for twenty-nine years. It was while at New College
he wrote arguably his greatest sacred work, an inspired
le-choir setting of words by one of the greatest of
sixteenth-century English poets, Edmund Spenser.
ctionately dedicated' to his predecessor at New College,
Hugh Allen, the setting is ravishing, with the original
ing adding to the ethereal atmosphere. Sadly, the original
uscript appears untraceable.

ource: Year Book Press (1925, revised 1948). *Variants:*
re slight differences occur between original piano
ction and voices, the voice parts have been followed.

Harwood: *O how glorious is the kingdom*

Harwood studied the organ both in England and at the
zig Conservatory, where his teachers included Carl

Reinecke (under whose directorship the Conservatory,
already one of the finest in Germany, was to become one of
the most renowned in Europe). On returning to Britain, he
was organist at the Church of St Barnabas Pimlico (1883–7),
Ely Cathedral (1887–92), and Christ Church College, Oxford
(1892–1909), at the same time holding the post of Precentor
of Keble College. Written in 1899, and dedicated to Rev.
H. A. Cumberlege, Vicar of Marston (a village just outside
Oxford), *O how glorious is the kingdom* displays the German
influence in the harmonies of the extravagant opening organ
prelude, complete with its chromatically rising build-up into
the spacious first chorus. Such an opening could easily have
formed the start of a large-scale organ or orchestral setting—
and indeed, Harwood did orchestrate the anthem. This
setting has long been a thrilling work for choirs to sing, and
no mean challenge for the organist too.

Source: Christ Church College, Oxford, MS 1247.
Variants: 4 iii 4: *d♮* required / 7 ii 10: *d♮* required / 12 ii 3–4:
original *d♮ d♮* progression (more Reger-esque, less homogen-
ized) is preferred to later printed versions / 23 vi 5: 'Ped.'
marking brought back by two quavers / 31 v 2 (upper voice):
g♯ required / 37 i 7: corrected in first printed edition to *d*.
Harwood's original note retained here / 38: double bar
editorial / 46: double bar editorial / 66 vi 6: *c♮* editorial.

18. Howells: *Like as the hart desireth the waterbrooks*

Herbert Howells was arguably the last of the true English
Romantics, fusing influences of Vaughan Williams, Delius,
Elgar, and others with his own unique melodic and,
especially, harmonic language. Having decided at an early age
that he would become a composer, he won a scholarship in
1912 to study composition at the Royal College of Music
with Stanford, where he also studied counterpoint with
Charles Wood. He returned to the RCM to teach in 1920 and
was still doing so fifty years later. Howells also served as
Director of Music at St Paul's Girls' School in London from
1936 to 1962, in succession to Holst, and in 1950 was
appointed professor at London University.

During 1941 Howells composed four anthems dedicated
to Sir Thomas Armstrong, who was at that time organist
at Christ Church, Oxford (Armstrong had succeeded William
Harris to that position). *Like as the hart* has subsequently
become one of the classics of English church music:
brilliantly written, it is as suitable for a novice choir as it is
for the finest of vocal ensembles. The autograph held at the
RCM shows that Howells, having completed his manuscript
(initialled and dated 'Cheltenham, 8 Jan: 1941'), reworked
his first ending the very same day by adding two bars after
b. 90, including a repeat of the words 'the presence'. The
autograph also reveals that the floating soprano descant
over the return of the first subject at b. 67 was a later
addition: in this edition the early version is provided as
an alternative. Other slight differences between the autograph
and the 1943 first printed edition include a handful of minor
repositionings of dynamics and two further minor rewritings
not here documented.

Source: First edition (OUP, 1943). Also consulted:
Autograph RCM MS 4601. *Variants:* 32 ii 2: dynamic taken
from autograph / 41 iv 2: 'ped.' added from autograph / 43:
position of crescendo taken from autograph / 63 iii 1:
dynamic taken from autograph / 63–7: position of *rall.*
molto al taken from autograph.

19. Ireland: *Greater love hath no man*

Born into a cultured family but losing both parents while in his early teens, Ireland was self-critical, often introspective, and a man to whom friendship meant a great deal. His music often reflects these characteristics. He studied composition at the Royal College of Music under Stanford and during his early career earned his living largely as organist of St Luke's, Chelsea, a post he held from 1904 to 1926. Having established himself in the front rank of composers, he returned to the RCM to teach composition, where his pupils included Britten and Moeran. *Greater love hath no man* was written in 1912, before the outbreak of the First World War, though its text could not have been more prophetic of the horrors that were soon to follow. The text was taken from seven carefully selected verses from the Bible: Song of Solomon 8: 7 & 6; John 15: 13; 1 Peter 2: 24; 1 Corinthians 6: 11; 1 Peter 2: 9; Romans 12: 1.

Source: First edition (Stainer & Bell, 1912). *Variants:* 20 vi 2: editorial staccato to match RH / 34 vi: *a♮* editorial to match RH (surely a printer's error).

20. Lewis: *The souls of the righteous*

Geraint Lewis studied music at St John's College, Cambridge, and since then has become a leading figure in presenting and writing music in his Welsh homeland. His anthem *The souls of the righteous* was written in memory of another Welsh composer, William Mathias, who had preceded Lewis as director of the North Wales Music Festival, and was first performed on 20 November 1992 in St Paul's Cathedral, conducted by John Scott. For this present volume the composer has revised the work, and suggests that the tempo should be adjusted according to the acoustic of each building. Conductors are also encouraged to use a little *rubato* to follow the natural flow of the music.

Source: Newly revised for this volume.

21. Mendelssohn: *Hear my prayer*

Mendelssohn's strong connections with the world of English choral music were lifelong. He visited Britain no fewer than ten times during his 38 years and was to become as favourite an adopted British composer as Handel. His studies of composers of the past were legendary: not just Bach, whom he championed, but Palestrina, Lassus, Handel, Boyce, and, thanks to his explorations of the library of Thomas Attwood, Purcell. Among the 'Psalms' of Purcell, as Mendelssohn described them, may well have been the astonishing setting of Psalm 55, which would surely have set a fertile mind such as Mendelssohn's racing. Purcell as catalyst or not, the genesis of Mendelssohn's own setting is worth exploring, for the anthem exists in several versions, with the text (as with many other of Mendelssohn's works, not least of all *Elias/Elijah*) in both German and English. *Hear my prayer* exists both with the composer's own organ accompaniment and in a version for full orchestra. The brief chronology is as follows: in November 1843, English lyrics were sent to Mendelssohn by his regular English librettist, William Bartholomew. The anthem was completed on 25 January 1844, but that autograph (held in the Deutsche Staatsbibliothek, Berlin) was unfortunately lost. A week later, Mendelssohn sent a second autograph to Bartholomew. This copy survives in London's Victoria and Albert Museum, with a beautifully written letter of dedication, but is so substantially different from the later

published version as to be only marginally useful in creati a new edition. Mendelssohn then offered the German versi for publication to Bote and Bock (dedicating the work Wilhelm Taubert, whose surname enabled a pun on 'Tau ('dove')), and the English version to Ewer & Co., and th turned to work on *Elijah*. During the rehearsals for th work, Mendelssohn was persuaded by the baritone solo Joseph Robinson, to create an orchestral version of *Hear prayer*, which was delivered in February 1847. And so at le five versions of the work were created but, frustratingly, source that would surely be of most interest no longer exi Instead, we must turn to the complete Mendelssohn editi compiled during the 1870s.

Source: Mendelssohns Werke (1874–7). Also consult BL Add. MS 46347 (orchestral score, 1847); Victoria Albert Museum 86.FF.50 (vocal score, 1844). *Method:* nc tion of accompaniment has been modernized without cc ment to follow modern conventions, though several origi disparities in beaming between voice and accompanim have been retained. Bartholomew's plethora of exclamat marks (b. 32 *et sim*) have been retained. *Variants:* 27 ii slur editorial / 36 iv 2: dynamic taken from orchestral sco 53 i 2: differs in length between orchestral and vocal sco but first edition shows ♩ / 70 v 1: printed as ♩ in vocal sc which causes harmonic collision; ♪ shown in orchestral sc therefore adopted / 97 iv 1: ♪ shown in orchestral sc adopted to match other voices / 138: source indic *Sostenuto* on second beat but both Add. MS 46347 86.FF.50 write *Sostenuto* | *a tempo* over first beat, whic adopted here.

22. Morley: *Nolo mortem peccatoris (I ask not the death of sinr*

Composer, editor, theorist, and organist, Morley wa remarkable musician, responsible more than anyone else the popularity of the Italian madrigal in England. Believe have been a pupil of William Byrd, he became organist c Paul's Cathedral, and was the composer of a signific corpus of sacred music. The motet *Nolo mortem pecca* appears in the 'Myriell' partbooks, a set copied by clergyman, compiler, and musical scribe Thomas My around 1616–20. The partbooks are an important, an some cases unique, source for the works of compe including Tomkins, Ferrabosco II, Peerson, Ward, and oth

Source: 'Myriell' partbooks, *Tristitiae Remed Cantiones selectissimae, diversorum tum autorum...*, BL MSS 29372–5. *Variants:* 39 iii 3: *c* in source corrected to avoid pairs of parallel fifths (though it could be argued such fifths were a musical pictorialization representing 'p / Punctuation throughout has been modernized.

23. Naylor: *Vox dicentis: Clama*

Naylor was born into a musical family: his father was org of York Minster. He became a choral scholar at Emma College, Cambridge, and later studied at the Royal Co of Music. After eight years as organist in various Lo churches he returned to Cambridge, where he taught at Leys School and also became organist of Emmanuel Col An early exponent of historical music practice, Naylor considered to be an authority on Shakespeare and m His substantial unaccompanied motet *Vox dicentis: C* was written in 1911 for the choir of King's Col Cambridge. The original manuscript is held in Emma llege library, but at the time of production of this volume s unavailable for viewing, due to the long-term closure of t library. Instead, this edition has been based on the first nted edition, dating from 1919, which Naylor oversaw. ylor provided an 'English paraphrase of the Latin original-et, adapted to the music as it stands'; for reasons of space s has been omitted in this edition. At times written in up eight parts, this grandly-scaled motet includes thematic terial that appears to be based on Gregorian chant.

Source: First edition (Curwen, 1919). *Method:* syllabic ts have been modernized without comment, as have ments of notation, spelling, and punctuation. *Variants:* 33 97: 'silent' over rests omitted / 173 ii: o altered to ♩♩ to ror two syllables of 'su-um' elsewhere.

Parsons: *Ave Maria (Honour we Mary)*

rces for this fine work are held in two Oxford libraries. five, beautifully copied 'Dow' partbooks in Christ rch College (c.1581–8) are less densely texted in 1–11, 43–8, and 52–8 than the sole part for second alto viving in the Bodleian Library (c.1575–89). As these leian text repetitions do not always coincide with the sical imitative points, however, it has been suggested that underlay may not have been the composer's work, and that the motet may be a reworking of an instrumental ce. Consequently, the five partbooks from Christ rch have been taken as the primary source, with the erlay in the three passages in question gently reconstruct-taking into account text repetitions from the (less florid) rano part as well as the inferences gleaned from the leian source. The aim has been to allow Parsons's glorious sma to flow freely while providing phrases of breathable ths.

ource: Christ Church College, Oxford, 'Dow' partbooks, s. 984–8. Also consulted: Bodleian Library, Oxford, MS s. Sch. 3. *Variants:* 12 i 1: o shortened to ♩ / 21 ii 1: ce has erroneous ♮ / 37 ii 3: source gives *f* / 64 i 3: ce gives *f*.

Philips: *Ascendit Deus (God has ascended)*

ugh born in London, and having been a chorister at St 's Cathedral, Peter Philips spent most of his adult life on continent, eventually settling in the Spanish Netherlands. ely considered to be a member of the school of Flemish posers, he nonetheless remained keen to describe himself nglish. A composer who was equally adept at writing oard music, instrumental settings, and both secular and ed music, he was widely published, surpassed only by iam Byrd. As its title would suggest, *Ascendit Deus* is a t for the feast of Pentecost. Along with the five vocal s here transcribed, the source, *Cantiones sacrae*, also ains a simple *basso continuo* part, which presents the st vocal line in use at that moment, with the addition of ndful of figures but no further cues. For this edition, a l reduction has been compiled, which could also be used e basis of an organ part, though most choirs nowadays this motet unaccompanied.

ource: Philips, *Cantiones sacrae, pro Propraecipuis Festis s anni et Communi Sanctorum* (Antwerp, 1612), British ary, BL K.7.a.7. *Method:* b. 50, triple section: time values d. *Variants:* 28 iii 2: erroneous ♯ removed / 38–49 iii: in ce texted 'Alleluia' but corrected to match other vocal

lines / 57: note lengths standardized / 60 i 3–61 i 1: source shows *e♮ f*.

26. Purcell: *Hear my prayer, O Lord*

Purcell's early autograph manuscript, now held in Cambridge's Fitzwilliam Museum, contains a remarkable collection of works by Blow, Gibbons, Locke, Child, Mundy, and others, as well as a dozen of Purcell's own works. He is a wonderful copyist: his inimitable, clear hand, elegant and rounded, is instantly readable. The manuscript includes a title page that contains the endearing comment: 'God bless Mr Henry Purcell / 1682 September the 10th'. The last anthem in the collection is *Hear my prayer*, which appears to be part of a larger piece that Purcell seemingly did not complete, for his barline at the end of the manuscript (going through the staves and not through the intervening spaces) is of the type that usually indicates that another section is to follow; indeed, he usually marks the end of a piece with an elaborate flourish. After this comes a number of blank pages. But we are fortunate to have this section of the anthem alone, for it is a masterpiece. Dating from 1680–2, its despairing text raises Purcell's imagination to its highest level, yet the basic melodic material is simple: two melancholy notes a minor third apart, countered by the plangent, turning chromaticism of 'crying'. The harmonic language is exceptional, even for Purcell, but the most extraordinary feature of the anthem is the build-up that Purcell orchestrates from the outset: an inexorable vocal crescendo lasting over three minutes, culminating on a monumental discord on the last repetition of 'come'.

Source: Fitzwilliam Museum, Cambridge, MS 88. *Method:* Purcell carefully places all textual slurs, here reproduced exactly. Cautionary accidentals are included except where made redundant by the modernized key signature. The organ continuo part is editorial. Original barring is every four minims: barlines have been added midway. Purcell's original ordering of the voices has been retained.

27. Purcell: *I was glad when they said unto me*

For the opulent coronation of James II on 23 April 1685, Purcell composed two new anthems: at the end of the service the combined choirs and orchestra performed the large-scale verse anthem *My heart is inditing*, and for the entrance of the King and Queen at the start of the service Purcell wrote this new setting of Psalm 122. James Hawkins, the eighteenth-century compiler of the 'Ely' Manuscript now held in Cambridge University Library (containing twenty-eight anthems, with eight attributed to Purcell, nine said to be by John Blow, and others by Turner, Tudway, Aldrich, Golding, Wise, and Hawkins himself), mistakenly ascribed the anthem on the title page to John Blow (though no composer is named within the actual manuscript). Only fairly recently has its authorship has been restored to Purcell.

As always, Purcell is a master of word-painting, from the joyful dotted figurations for 'glad', the assembly of the various 'tribes of the Lord', the central supplicatory mood, to an exultant Gloria. In this final compositional tour de force, the four-note descending imitative point is first treated conventionally, then in inversion, then in inverted augmentation in the bass line. Finally, as the sopranos and altos contest the theme at the original speed in real and inverted form, with the tenors in single inverted augmentation, the basses triumphantly halve even this speed to present Purcell's theme in double augmentation.

Source: Cambridge University Library, 'Ely' manuscript, EDC 10/7/6. *Method:* The manuscript is neat, with every accidental individually marked, even when these occur on successive notes, indicating that when an accidental within a bar is not re-marked, a reversion to the non-accidental is intended. b. 57 original time signature ¢, barred in 4 beats per bar / b. 63 original time signature **31**; note values here halved and barred in 3 beats per bar / b. 86 original time signature ¢, barred 4 beats per bar. Variants: 94 v 7: source gives *f♮*, here altered to match imitation in the other vocal lines.

28. Purcell: *Let mine eyes run down with tears*

This sacred masterpiece dates from around 1682, and vividly demonstrates Purcell's mastery of word setting. Jeremiah's desolate text is treated to a rich five-part vocal texture, with the composer's graphic harmonic and melodic language at its most original. Vivid pictorialization is present in almost every phrase and word, from the opening downward melisma, representing tears, through the desolate setting of 'broken', the false relation on 'great breach', and the scotch snap to the jagged downward leap for 'very grievous blow'. In the recitative-like section there is notable word-painting for 'sick', before the voices unite for a pathos-laden 'Hast thou utterly rejected Judah? hath thy soul loath'd Zion?'. 'Why hast thou smitten us' is mournfully, almost angrily, passed between the voices, uniting at 'And there is no healing for us?'. The simplicity of the first chorus comes as a relief from such tensions, but desolation quickly returns, with pleading repetitions by each voice of 'remember' and the anguished 'O do not disgrace the throne of thy glory'. Finally, a more optimistic mood emerges at 'Art thou not he', before the final chorus, instructed in the manuscript 'Triple again for ye chorus & so conclude', gives grounds for optimism.

Source: Autograph, Bodleian Library, Oxford, Mus. C.26.f.4 (MS 16702). *Method:* Capitalization of original underlay has been standardized in line with modern conventions, as has spelling. All vocal slurs are original. Continuo line is original except first chorus (bb. 51–65). Continuo figuring is predominantly editorial. b. 96: Purcell's six-beat bars are here halved in length.

29. Purcell: *Lord, how long wilt thou be angry?*

Another anthem from Purcell's autograph 'Fitzwilliam' manuscript, and dating from the early 1680s, this is a marvellous synthesis of old and new compositional styles. The five-part imitative opening choral section reflects the influence on Purcell's music of the generation of Byrd and Gibbons, and over this traditional form Purcell imprints his own angularly chromatic harmonic language. The three-voice verse section is reflective, descending to 'great misery'. The homophonic chorus 'Help us, O God' is declamatory, and 'for the glory of thy Name' impressively builds its close entries before the opening imitative style returns for 'O deliver us', still coloured by chromatic lines that rise through 'and be merciful unto our sins'. The anthem closes with a joyful triple-time movement.

Source: Fitzwilliam Museum, Cambridge, MS 88. *Method:* Textual slurs are original. Purcell is meticulous in their placing, as he is with cautionary accidentals. The continuo part is entirely editorial. The original barring contains four beats per bar, here halved. b. 77: original time signature with ⊙ prolation. Note values halved and original barr[ing] halved in length. Variants: 84 v 1: original length ♩.

30. Purcell: *Remember not, Lord, our offences*

This five-part full anthem is another remarka[ble] demonstration of Purcell's use of harmony and discord, startlingly effective word-setting, and his mastery of dra[ma]. The atmosphere is created from the first word, set as a sim[ple] block chord, then reiterated as the phrase moves forward [to] 'offences'. The first touches of counterpoint appear at '[wi]th'offences of our forefathers', and the tension starts [to] increase with 'neither take thou vengeance of our si[ns]', always countered in at least one other voice with the ris[ing] 'but spare us, good Lord'. Gradually the calls for mercy, 'spare us', begin to dominate, and the chromaticism a[nd] daring use of discord increases: the music reaches a clim[ax] with a desperate plea, 'spare us, good Lord'. Quickly [the] mood returns to supplication: Purcell's harmony rela[xes] deliciously onto 'redeem'd' and the tenors' dominant seve[nth] clashes exquisitely with a second inversion chord [on] 'precious'. It is the tenors again who have a wonderf[ully] subtle inner line at 'for ever' and, after such passion, [the] anthem ends, as it began, with a calm prayer for salvatio[n].

Source: Fitzwilliam Museum, Cambridge, MS 88. *Meth[od:]* A slightly less tidy copy than some others in the 'Fitzwilli[am]' volume, textual slurs are nevertheless clearly indicated. L[ines] 1 and 5 are fully texted in the manuscript, with the mid[dle] three lines, when in homophony, only cued. No t[ime] signature is given. The continuo part is entirely edito[rial.] *Variants:* 3 iv: source self-corrects underlay to that given [here] / 44 ii: source notates ♩ ♩. (against the ◖◗ of the other voic[es]).

31. Stainer: *God so loved the world*

This chorus, from the much-loved *The Crucifixion*—a w[ork] for chorus, soloists, and organ, first performed in 1887 [and] described by Stainer as 'A Meditation on the Sacred Pas[sion] of the Holy Redeemer'—remains one of the staples of English Victorian musical tradition. Stainer was one of [the] first of the modern generation of musicologists, m[uch] admired in his day as a choir trainer. His compositions h[ave] mostly not survived the test of time, and in later life he [was] dismissive of most of them, stating that he wished they [had] not been published. *The Crucifixion* nevertheless remai[ns a] much-performed work, and *God so loved the world*, ca[st in] simple ternary form with coda, is probably its most fam[ous] movement.

Source: First edition (Novello, *c.*1890).

32. Stainer: *I saw the Lord*

Stainer was a chorister at St Paul's Cathedral and in 1[?] sang as a soloist in the first English performance of Bach['s] *Matthew Passion*. After his voice changed he bec[ame] organist at St Benedict and St Peter's Church, Paul's Wh[arf,] and also played on occasion at St Paul's Cathedral, whe[re in] 1856 Sir Frederick Ouseley heard him playing the organ [and] offered him the post of organist at the newly founded co[llege] of St Michael's, Tenbury. While in Tenbury, in 1858, [the] 18-year-old Stainer composed his anthem for Tr[inity] Sunday—his only sacred work for double choir—with a [text] that combined verses from Isaiah with a verse fro[m an] eleventh-century Latin hymn. The dramatic opening

sequent pauses suggest that the generous acoustic of St
ul's remained in his mind. Stainer later went on to study at
ford, was appointed organist at Magdalen College aged
y 20, became organist of St Paul's Cathedral in 1872, and
led his professional career back in Oxford as Professor of
sic (1889–99).

Source: First edition (Novello). Also consulted:
tograph, Tenbury MS 1352 (Bodleian Library, Oxford).
thod: Originally notated with a basic ♩ pulse, in the style
Renaissance works; note values have been halved. The
ginal manuscript layout is SSAATTBB, but the later
nted edition shows a double-choir layout. *Variants:* 7 ii:
s *a* in autograph adopted in preference to *f* in first edition
28–35: printed edition has 'seraphims'; autograph
aphim' adopted / 54: ♩. in choir 1 and ♩ in choir 2 is
ginal / 87 x: accents editorially added in LH / 89 v 1:
cing of 'Con Ped.' under fourth beat implies that beats 1–3
manuals / 92 vi 1 & 3: accents here omitted.

Stanford: *Beati quorum via (How blessed are faithful souls)*

nford was born in Dublin. Aged 18 he won a scholarship
Queens' College, Cambridge, and at the age of only 21 was
ointed organist of Trinity College. He studied in Germany
n Reinecke and Kiel, travelled widely, met both Brahms
Offenbach, and was present at the opening of Wagner's
reuth Festival Theatre. His reputation as a composer
w, and in 1883, having resigned his post at Trinity, he was
le Professor of Composition at the Royal College of Music,
owed four years later by his appointment as Professor
Music at Cambridge, still aged only 35. Best known
adays for his prodigious output of canticles, anthems,
motets, which rightly still enjoy their places in the
ertoire of any leading cathedral choir, he also composed a
stantial corpus of orchestral works, including seven
phonies. His legacy as a teacher was also considerable,
h his pupils numbering almost every major English
poser of the era, including Bliss, Bridge, Gurney, Holst,
vells, Ireland, Lambert, and Vaughan Williams. Stanford's
ee Latin Motets, Op. 38, were dedicated to Alan Gray, his
essor at Trinity, and the Choir of Trinity College,
ibridge. Offered to Novello for publication in 1888, they
e turned down and not published until 1905.

rce: First edition (Boosey, 1905). *Variants:* 39 ii 1: tied to
bar in source but with a new text syllable and slur (as
transcribed), so likely to be a printer's error.

Stanford: *Coelos ascendit hodie (Heaven receives Lord today)*

second of Stanford's *Three Latin Motets*, this is an
nsiontide setting that makes much of the interplay
veen the two choirs. The final 'Amen', with all the voices
ing on a single note, spreads brilliantly outwards.

ource: First edition (Boosey, 1905).

Stanford: *How beauteous are their feet*

ng his last years, Stanford's income from the Royal
ege of Music dwindled, and he became increasingly
ndent on royalties from his published works. The result
a return to the composition of smaller works: songs,
s for both organ and violin, and church music, including
923 this 'Short Anthem for Saints' Days'.

ource: First edition (Novello, 1923).

36. Stanford: *I heard a voice from heaven*

Into this setting of a verse from the Book of Revelation,
especially suitable for the commemoration of the dead,
Stanford incorporates part of the medieval melody 'Angelus
ad virginem', which he states had been given to him by the
scholar and Cambridge University Librarian Henry Bradshaw
in 1883.

Source: First edition (Novello, 1910).

37. Stanford: *Justorum animae (The hand of God holds faithful souls)*

We know that this fine work, the first of Stanford's *Three
Latin Motets*, with its contemplative outer sections and vivid
central part, was performed at evensong at Trinity College,
Cambridge, on 24 February 1888. Stanford wrote to his
prospective publisher that all three motets were used
frequently at Trinity, both in chapel and as grace anthems in
college hall before dinner.

Source: First edition (Boosey, 1905).

38. Tallis: *Loquebantur variis linguis*

In this complex, seven-part Latin motet, setting the respond
on the plainchant for First Vespers at Pentecost, with the
chant in the tenor, Tallis produces a wonderfully rich vocal
texture, the waves of sound surely meant to represent all the
Apostles speaking at once in their newly acquired tongues.
Tallis's trademark false relations (the simultaneous sounding
of both flattened and raised leading notes, for instance in bb.
9 and 11) add to the wonderfully harmonious depiction of
linguistic cacophony.

Both sources are copied by anthologist, composer, and
singer John Baldwin (d. *c.*1615). Baldwin was a tenor lay
clerk at St George's Chapel, Windsor, from 1575, and later a
Gentleman of the Chapel Royal, and is perhaps best known
as the copyist of *My Ladye Nevells Booke*, containing
keyboard pieces by William Byrd. At first glance, his full
score (held in the British Library) appears as if it is in eight
parts, but Baldwin started the first bass part a bar too late,
only realizing his mistake at b. 28. Being the last part to be
written into the fair copy, the erroneous passage is not
crossed out, but instead written out correctly one stave lower.
All students of palaeography who have made a similar
mistake should take heart that even those for whom such
copies were daily bread and butter in the sixteenth century
could count their rests wrongly and spoil a manuscript.

Source: Christ Church College, Oxford, MSS 979–83
(contains five of the voices), *c.*1575–81. Also consulted (for
tenor and bass 2): BL RM 24.d.2 (in score, wordless).
Variants: Plainsong sections editorially reconstructed /
Position of bass voices reversed to place lower bass voice
below upper bass / 8 v 1: source shows o / 39 v 1: source
shows ♩ ♩

39. Tallis: *O Lord, give thy Holy Spirit*

This work, which mixes syllabic setting with sections of
gentle imitation and counterpoint, was circulated widely:
three manuscripts are held in the British Library, and further
versions exist in the libraries of Tenbury, Gloucester, Ely, and
York. As late as 1715 the work was still in the repertoire, and
was included in the six thick quarto volumes compiled by
Thomas Tudway, Professor of Music at Cambridge, at the
behest of Edward, Lord Harley, the second Earl of Oxford.

The 'Harley' manuscript is notable as being the work of one of the first ardent music researchers seeking out the rich heritage of English sacred music contained in the cathedral libraries. The earliest manuscript, held in the British Library, gives us the first evidence of the shorter version of the first-time bar (in some later manuscripts the voices settle together on a minim before the soprano restarts), and has created the basis for this edition, with the second voice taken from a manuscript dating from around 1625, and the third and fourth voices taken from later sources. The organ part is editorial, created as a reduction of the vocal parts.

Sources: BL Add. MS 15166 (*c*.1567, voice 1); BL Add. MS 29289 (*c*.1625, voice 2); BL Add. MS 30478 (*c*.1640, voice 3); Lbl. Harley MS 7337 (*c*.1715, voice 4). *Variants:* 21 i 1: source gives ♩.

40. Tallis: *O nata lux de lumine (O holy light once born of light)*
In 1575, having petitioned Queen Elizabeth for some source of additional income, Tallis and Byrd were granted an exclusive licence to print and publish music. This resulted, later that year, in the publication of *Cantiones sacrae*, to which each contributed seventeen works, perhaps reflecting the same number as Elizabeth's years on the throne. Among Tallis's numbers came this little jewel, exemplifying why he was so respected not only by his contemporaries but by many succeeding generations of composers.

Source: Thoma Tallisio & Guilielmo Birdo, *Cantiones, quae ab argumento sacrae vocantur* (1575), BL K.3.f.9. *Variants:* Key signature for superius made consistent with the other four parts / 2 ii 2: there is no authority for the e♮ found in many editions.

41. Tallis: *If ye love me*
Tallis lived through one of the more turbulent periods of English religious history and needed to write in whatever musical style was required at that moment. For the Protestants in the reign of Edward VI this consisted of simple, syllabic settings with every word clearly audible; for the Catholics under Mary it was complex textures with Latin words; and during the reign of Elizabeth I a musical halfway house emerged where the texts could still be heard but the music could nonetheless remain interesting. It is Tallis's skill at adapting so naturally to each phase that shows his consummate musical craftsmanship. *If ye love me* is a fine demonstration of his skill in the first category, its dating from before 1548 confirmed by inclusion in a now incomplete set of partbooks held in Oxford's Bodleian Library. For this edition we have turned to the earliest complete set of partbooks, published during Tallis's lifetime and thus presumably authoritative.

Source: John Day, *Certaine notes set forth in foure and three parts...* (London, 1560), BL K.7.E.7 (*Medius & Bassus* parts only); John Day, *Mornyng and Evenyng prayer and Communion, set forth in foure parts...* (London, 1565), BL K.7.E.8. *Variants:* 20: the word 'spirit' is original, but so as to occupy one syllable, rather than the modern two, performers may wish to pronounce it as 'sprit' / 26 iii 1: source gives *c*, which produces such obvious parallel fifths with the bass that this has to be a printing error.

42. Taverner: *Dum transisset Sabbatum*
This motet, a setting of the third respond at Matins on Easter Sunday, survives in two sources, both held in the library Christ Church College, Oxford. That copied by John Baldw (see Tallis, *Loquebantur variis linguis*) lacks the cantus firm (first bass) part, but Baldwin is regarded by many scholars being the less likely of the two copyists to make his o additions or alterations (the other copyist, Robert Dow, v an Oxford scholar). Similarities between Baldwin and Do manuscripts suggest that, though both were copied more t thirty years after the composition, they may have been ba on the same source: both insert the words of the plainsong incipit under the opening choral polypho (though it does not fit that music) and neither gives subsequent plainsong sections. The full form of the p requires a plainsong incipit and the first complete cho polyphony, then the first plainsong verse 'et valde man followed by the polyphony from 'Ut venientes', and fin the plainsong doxology (the Gloria) and the choral 'allelu During the 1960s the scholar Philip Brett sugges reconstructing the plainsong sections by reference to *Sarum Antiphoner* printed in Paris during Taverner's lifeti and the opening incipit from indications in the Gyffard p books (British Library Add. MSS 17802–5), a solution this edition also follows.

Source: Christ Church College, Oxford, MSS 979 (copied by John Baldwin). Also consulted: MSS 984–8 (h of Robert Dow). *Variants:* 6 v 6: Baldwin writes ♪♪♩/ 32 Baldwin writes ♪♪ (presumably 'al-le-'), whereas Dow g ♪, which better fits imitation elsewhere.

43. Tomkins: *When David heard*
The last English representative of the Renaissance schoo composers, Thomas Tomkins was conservative to the and has more anthems and services to his name than other composer except for William Child—a statistic which his son Nathaniel can take much of the credit, tha to his publication in 1668 of large quantities of his fat work in *Musica Deo Sacra*. Tomkins was clearly held in regard, for his works were widely distributed in manusc Where the primary source of this anthem, printed durin composer's lifetime, has unclear underlay due to repetition signs or printed words not quite aligning notes, the 1616 handwritten copy has been consulted. 1668 copy, written in 'short' score with the text cued in a start of phrases, is the only source with a keyboard part, was published after Tomkins's death and contains a num of errors. The anthem in the 1622 collection is dedicated Mr Thomas Myriell' (see Byrd, *Sing joyfully* and Mo *Nolo mortem peccatoris*).

Source: Thomas Tomkins, *Songs of 3. 4. 5. and 6. I* (London, 1622), BL. K.3.K.7. Also consulted: *Musica Sacra* (*c*.1616), BL Add MSS 29372–6; Thomas Tom *Musica Deo Sacra* (1668). *Variants:* 30 ii 3: rhythm of preferred to ♩. ♪ given in 1622 edition.

44. Vaughan Williams: *O how amiable are thy dwelling*
The finest composer of his generation, Vaughan Will studied in Britain with Parry, Wood, and Stanford, abroad with both Bruch and Ravel. Despite being agnostic, he contributed a substantial quantity of fine ch music to the repertoire, including this anthem, originally of the music he wrote for the Abinger Pageant of 1 Abinger was a village near his childhood home in Surrey.

geant was held in aid of the Abinger Church Preservation
nd, and the anthem was dedicated to Frances Farrar,
first secretary of the Abinger Women's Institute. The text,
l the inclusion of the hymn O God our help in ages past,
ke it especially suitable for festivals or for the dedication
a church.

Source: First edition (OUP, 1940). *Variants:* 40 iii 4: upper
ord corrected to match b. 36.

Vaughan Williams: *O taste and see*

the 1950s Vaughan Williams was the grand old man of
glish music, with a massive corpus of music behind him.
had developed a truly English voice across an
raordinarily broad output. At the time of the coronation
Elizabeth II on 2 June 1953, Vaughan Williams, now aged
was still an extremely active musician, with two of his
e symphonies ahead of him; he had recently completed
at was to be his final stage work, *The Pilgrim's Progress*.
contribution to such a grand coronation was a typically
erstated and modest 'Motet for unaccompanied choir
n organ introduction'.

Source: First edition (OUP, 1953).

Walton: *Set me as a seal upon thine heart*

ton's early compositional career did not earn him any
stantial income until he began to write music for films in
1930s, and he was greatly helped before that time by the
erosity of a number of friends and admirers, including
ert and Sacheverell Sitwell, and Lady Wimborne. When
22 November 1938 the Wimbornes' eldest son, the
nourable Ivor Guest (at that time Member of Parliament
Brecon and Radnor), married Lady Mabel Fox-
ngways, daughter of the sixth Earl of Ilchester, Walton
te this delectable setting of glorious words from the Song
olomon.

Source: First edition (OUP, 1938).

Wesley: *Blessed be the God and Father*

uel Sebastian Wesley is a fascinating character. The son of
uel Wesley (his middle name given in homage to his
er's hero, Bach), he became arguably the finest English
poser of church music since Purcell at a time when
ical standards in cathedrals had sunk to a deplorable
. Few cathedral chapters were willing to devote any
urces to music, and Wesley fought tirelessly to counter
r musical standards, constantly complaining of
nteeism and incompetence among the adult singers, poor
ns, and inadequate rehearsal time. He was not afraid to
ge with the cathedral authorities in each of the jobs he
, moving through Hereford, Exeter, Leeds, Winchester,
finally Gloucester; but away from the battles his positive
enge to all these choirs was to produce a magnificent
s of anthems and canticles. For Easter Sunday at
ford, probably around 1835, he wrote this splendid
ng. Its middle section, with the solo soprano answered by
tutti sopranos, is typically melodious, and equally
ally unconventional in its irregular phrase structure. At
rst performance the anthem may well have failed to show
ll potential, for the forces available proved to be only the
es of the choir and a solitary bass singer, who outside the
dral doubled as the Dean's butler.

ource: First edition (Hall Virtue, 1853).

48. Wesley: *Praise the Lord, O my soul*

Wesley's larger-scale pieces are nowadays rarely performed,
which is much to be regretted, for these are fine works. *Praise
the Lord, O my soul* was written (to mark the opening of a
new small organ) while Wesley was at Winchester, and makes
few concessions to the singers, at one point moving into nine
voice parts. A trademark Wesley technique is intermittently to
send his altos—who were of course male falsettists—into
'chest' register. Wesley notated these passages in the bass clef,
but for modern-day altos this edition notates them in 'treble
octave' clef. The middle section celebrates the new organ with
a particularly ornate part, but it is the closing chorus, coming
after a strong, chorale-like section, that has brought the piece
everlasting fame. Here placed in its true context, 'Lead me,
Lord' takes on an entirely new aspect.

Source: First edition (Hall Virtue, 1872). *Variants:* 5–12
vi: lower octave removed where it falls below modern organ
compass / 24 iii 1: e♭ implied / 29 v & 33 iii: e♭ implied / 103
ii 16: ♮ to *d* editorial / 105 ii 4: source erroneously gives *b* ♯/
121 ii 16: ♮ to *d* editorial / 124 v 5: ♯ editorial / 130 v 3: ♮ to
lower *g* editorial / 145 ix 2: ♮ to lower *g* editorial / 152 iii 5:
♭ editorial / 154 iii 3: ♮ to *g* editorial / 155 iv 1:♮ to *c* editorial
/ 160 v 2: source gives erroneous dot on ♩ / 160 v 4: ♮ to
editorial / 161 v 3: ♮ to *c* editorial / 163 v 4: ♮ to *g* editorial /
163 vi 4: ♮ to *c* editorial / 172 vi: ♩. added editorially to match
b. 96 / 194 iv 1: ♮ to *g* editorial / 197 iv 2: ♮ to *g* editorial /
214 iv 1:♮ to *g* editorial / 215 i 1: ♮ to *g* editorial.

49. Wesley: *Thou wilt keep him in perfect peace*

Also dating from Wesley's Winchester period comes this little
jewel, probably written around 1850. The eight gentle bars of
opening material, reiterated at the midpoint and at the end,
create a framework for two more adventurous sections.
Wesley retains one final surprise for the penultimate bar,
imaginatively resolving a splendidly unexpected discord back
into gentle consonance.

Source: First edition (Hall Virtue, 1853). Returning to this
earliest reputable source allows the removal of later editorial
additions, particularly with regard to the organ part.
Variants: 4 vii 1: LH crotchet printed as *e*, but as is *g* in
subsequent reprises and in the tenor above, it is here
corrected / 61 vii 4: slur omitted.

50. Wesley: *Wash me throughly*

Written probably while Wesley was at Exeter—a cathedral
that Wesley was later to say he regretted leaving—*Wash me
throughly* is another near-perfect short anthem: beautifully
constructed, melodious, compact in its use of musical
material, and expressive. Returning to this earliest reputable
source helps remove a handful of later editorial additions.
None of the manuscripts from which the 1853 collection was
engraved are known to survive, and it has to be assumed that
they were not returned to Wesley, who appears to have
retained any manuscript returned to him after publication.

Source: First edition (Hall Virtue, 1853). *Variants:* 1–2 &
9–10: soprano *cresc.* & *dim.* added editorially to make consistent with organ and match tenor at 64–5 / 87 vi 1: dots
removed from both ♩ to standardize to other parts / 97–8 vi:
organ LH transposed up octave to remain within modern
pedal compass.

51. Wood: *O thou the central orb*

The Irish-born Charles Wood studied with Bridge, Stanford, and Parry at the Royal College of Music. He moved to Cambridge to become organist at Selwyn College, then at Gonville and Caius, where in 1894 he was made a fellow. Three years later he was appointed as a university lecturer in music, and on the death of Stanford in 1924 was made professor. A fine composer, and a fastidious teacher whose pupils included both Vaughan Williams and Howells, he turned increasingly during his later years to the composition of sacred music, writing six settings of the evening canticles and some equally well-crafted anthems, including, in 1915,

this setting of a hymn by the Oxford cleric and acade[m] Henry Ramsden Bramley. Returning to Wood's manuscr[ipt] enables the correction of a long-standing error made by [the] original typesetter, who misread Wood's handwritten 'clay' [in] b. 60 as 'day', and which early proofreaders failed to no[te makes little linguistic or rhymed sense.

Source: Autograph manuscript, Library of Gonville [and] Caius College, Cambridge, Wood envelope 19i. *Varia[nts:]* Wood's slurring of pairs of quavers has been followed in [the] organ part but, following modern convention, has b[een] standardized in the vocal parts.

INDEX OF ORCHESTRATIONS

Scores and parts of the following anthems are available on rental from the publisher or copyright owner (as indicated).

16.   Hadley: My song is love unknown (OUP)
2fl, 2ob, 2cl, 2bsn, 4hn, 2tpt, 3tbn, timp, hp, organ (*ad lib.*), str

19.   Ireland: Greater love hath no man (Stainer & Bell Ltd)
2fl, 2ob, 2cl, 2bsn, 4hn, 3tpt, 3tbn, tba, timp, organ, str

21.   Mendelssohn: Hear my prayer (OUP)
2fl, 2ob, 2cl, 2bsn, 2hn, timp, str

44.   Vaughan Williams: O how amiable are thy dwellings (OUP)
organ, str

An accompaniment for brass ensemble (2tpt, hn, tbn, tba), percussion, and organ is available on sale from the pub[lisher] (ISBN 978-0-19-386250-0).

Continuo parts with figured bass for bowed and plucked continuo instruments (cello, bass violin, viola da gamba, theorbo[,]are available to purchase as a single volume through the OUP hire library:

4.   Boyce: O where shall wisdom be found?
14.   Greene: Lord, let me know mine end
26.   Purcell: Hear my prayer, O Lord
27.   Purcell: I was glad when they said unto me
28.   Purcell: Let mine eyes run down with tears
29.   Purcell: Lord, how long wilt thou be angry?
30.   Purcell: Remember not, Lord, our offences